Master Studies II

by Joe Morello

Edited by Marvin Burock

Transcribed by Sam Ruttenberg & Marvin Burock

Project Coordinator: Bill Miller

Photography by Andrew Lepley

Published by
Modern Drummer Publications, Inc.
12 Old Bridge Road
Cedar Grove, NJ 07009

Dedication

To my dear wife, Jean Ann, for your love, support,
and inspiration throughout the years.

This book is also dedicated in memoriam to my friend, Ron Spagnardi.

Acknowledgements

I would like to express my sincere thanks to Marvin Burock,
Jim Jacobus, Sam Ruttenberg, Mauricio de Souza, John Riley, and
Bill Miller, whose invaluable assistance helped to make this book a reality.

Contents

Foreword

by John Riley

"You've gone as far as you can go with the technique you're using. If you do as I say, practicing three or four hours every day, in three months you'll improve your sound, play more relaxed, and double your speed."

Sitting behind me on the plane ride home from the 1971 Ludwig Drum Symposium, at the University of Miami, were a couple of other participants about my age. They had their sticks out and were practicing on the back of my seat. These guys were playing some wicked stuff, so I asked them who they studied with. They—Danny Gottlieb and Bobby Muskus—lived a couple towns away from me and studied with Joe Morello, who, unbeknownst to me, taught twenty minutes from my house. I had attended Joe's classes at the workshop, along with those of Roy Haynes, Alan Dawson, Gary Burton, Carmine Appice, and Bobby Christian. But the symposium was a hundred-hour whirlwind in drum heaven, and Joe's classes were kind of a blur in my saturated memory. Danny encouraged me to study with Joe.

I made an appointment for an "evaluation" and arrived early at Dorn And Kirshner Music in Union, New Jersey. I was directed upstairs to a large room full of sheet music, a closed door with "Joe Morello" on it, and a small waiting room—not a typical waiting room, for it contained a metronome, three or four chairs, and some very well-worn practice pads. I nervously entered and was eagerly greeted by a couple of guys blistering those pads. They told me I was in the right place; they too were students of Joe's, and he was the greatest.

Finally my time came. Joe invited me into his studio and asked me to sit at the practice pad to his left. The wall directly in front of us was mirrored. Behind us was Joe's drumkit. He had me play a single-stroke roll, a double-stroke roll, paradiddles, and some other rudiments, and read a bit from the Wilcoxon and Cirone books, none of which I had any problems with. Joe joined in on a couple of the elements and startled me when he used his right hand to push his glasses up his nose but continued to play just as fast with only his left hand as I was with both hands. Then he very gently gave me his evaluation. "You've gone as far…."

I took the first available lesson slot and began the process of relearning how to move the sticks. Practicing was no problem because Joe's method was very clear and my improvement was rapid. Several afternoons a week I would go directly from my high school to the shop, spending hours in the waiting room practicing with other students. The situation was ideal. I became immersed in Joe's methods. I guess he saw my dedication and progress, because he was very generous, often sneaking me in for a quick five-minute check-up and pep talk between my regular weekly lessons.

The primary text used was George L. Stone's *Stick Control*. Joe had me do very specific exercises at precise tempos and dynamic levels. In a very short time my hands started to feel, react, and sound better. We played through Stone dozens of different ways, many of which became the foundation for Joe's fantastic book, *Master Studies*. I was fortunate to have had ten months of weekly lessons before I left for college. Now, over thirty years later, a day doesn't go by that I am not reminded of something Joe taught me. He changed my relationship to the drums, and that changed my life.

Joe's teaching methods have continued to evolve and expand. With the much anticipated release of *Master Studies II*, we can all enjoy an additional dose of wisdom from a master. If you practice this material as prescribed, you too can improve your sound, play more relaxed, and double your speed. I did. Thanks, Joe.

Introduction

by Joe Morello

It seems like just yesterday that *Master Studies* was first published. I can hardly believe that it's been more than twenty years. I hope you enjoy *Master Studies II*. In many respects, this book picks up where the original *Master Studies* left off. Some of the material shown here is more difficult than that found in the first book. Like *Master Studies*, it's a workbook of material to use in developing the hands. It is not a drumset or coordination book, although several of the exercises can be played on the drumset. This book can be used by the classical, jazz, rock, or even rudimental drummer, although it does not focus on the rudiments as such.

Many of the exercises found in this book can be played in a variety of ways. For example, several can be played as written or with a jazz feel. The whole idea is to play these exercises in a musical fashion. They should also be practiced with varied dynamic levels. Furthermore, this book does not have to be practiced in any particular order. You can skip around and work on whichever sections are most important to your needs at any given time.

The exercises in this book should be practiced with a metronome. It will help you to play more rhythmically accurate by teaching you to space the notes correctly. The metronome can also be used to track your progress. As your proficiency increases, you can play with the metronome set at higher tem-

pos. I suggest starting off slowly each time you practice, making sure that you remain totally relaxed. After your muscles are warmed up, you can gradually increase the tempo.

As I mentioned in *Master Studies*, I have come to the conclusion that everything is done with natural body movement. The wrist turns and other movements have to be natural; they have to fit the way the body is made. You must use everything in a natural way. After you've been playing for a while, you'll develop an individualized style, and each style has its place.

Some of the exercises are very challenging to play and require slow, sensible, and accurate practice. Please be patient. The results will be more than satisfying. In my teaching, I have given many of these exercises to my students, and they have worked wonders. Always remember that technique is only a means to an end. The ultimate goal is to play musically. You have to apply the technique to the music you are playing. It's up to you to use your imagination and develop your own ideas. This book is meant to help further develop your facility, keep you in shape, and help you become aware of what your hands are doing and how they are working. How you use the technique is up to you. Good luck!

Warm-Up Exercises

The following three exercises can be played at the start of each practice session. They are designed to loosen your muscles as well as build control and endurance. Try playing a few different lines each day, repeating each ten times. Practice slowly at first, and remember to remain relaxed at all times. Eventually you should be able to play each exercise in its entirety. These exercises can be played as shown or using only the right or left hand.

Warm-Up Exercise 1

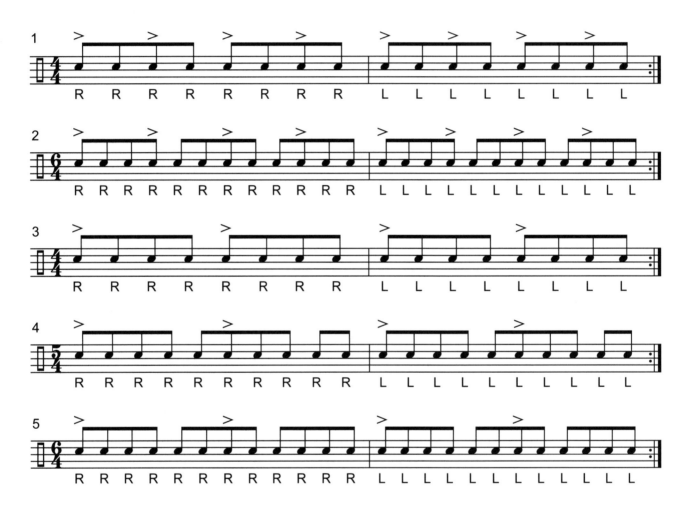

Warm-Up Exercise 2

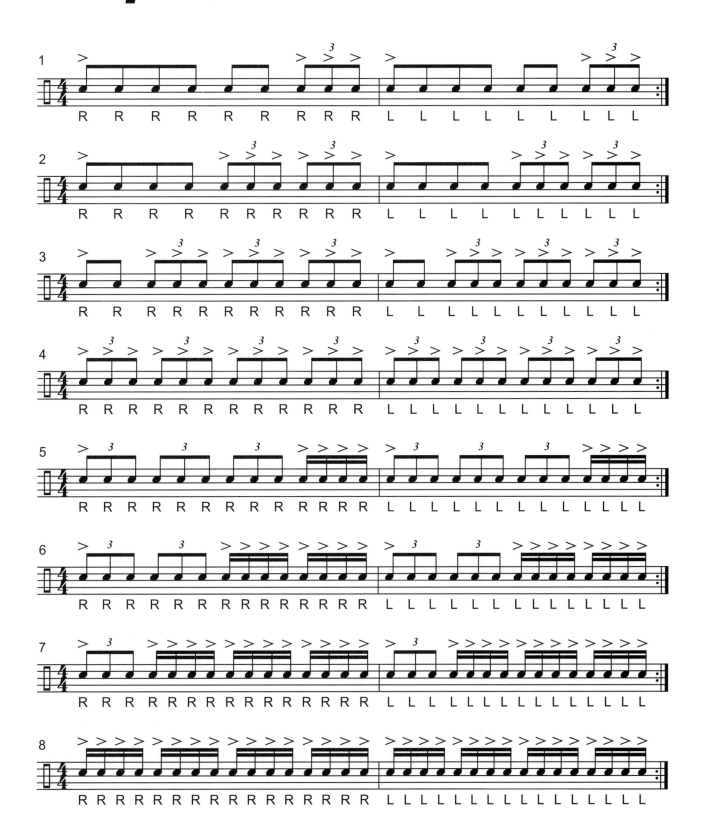

Warm-Up Exercise 3

8th-Note And Triplet Combinations

The following exercises can be played as written, i.e., in their classical or "legitimate" form, where the 8th note is given its true value. They can also be played using an 8th-note-triplet (or jazz) feel, as shown in the first (smaller) example below. Use your imagination to create different phrasings by adding accents. Also feel free to experiment with varied dynamic levels.

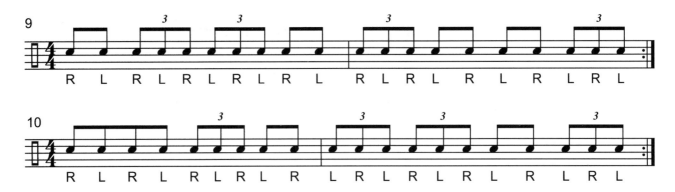

The following is a variation of the previous exercise using groups of six in single strokes. These are great for building your single-stroke-roll chops.

8 RLRLRLRL RLRLRLRLRLRLRLRLRLRLRL

9 RLRLRLRLRLRLRLRLRL L RLRLRLRLRLRL R LRLRL

10 RLRLRLRLRLRL RLRLRLRLRLRLR L RLRLRL

The following exercise is similar to the previous one, only now we're using double strokes instead of single strokes on each group of six.

1 RL RRLLRRL R LLRRLL RL RRLLRRL R LLRRLL

2 RLRL RRLLRRLLRRLL RLRL RRLLRRLLRRLL

3 RL RRLLRRL R LLRRLL RRLLRRL R LLRRLLR L

4 RLRRLLRRLRLR LLRRLLR L RRLLRRLLRRLL

5 RL RRLLRRL R LLRRLL RLRL RRLLRRLLRRLL

6 RL R L R L RRLLRR L R L R L R LLRRLL

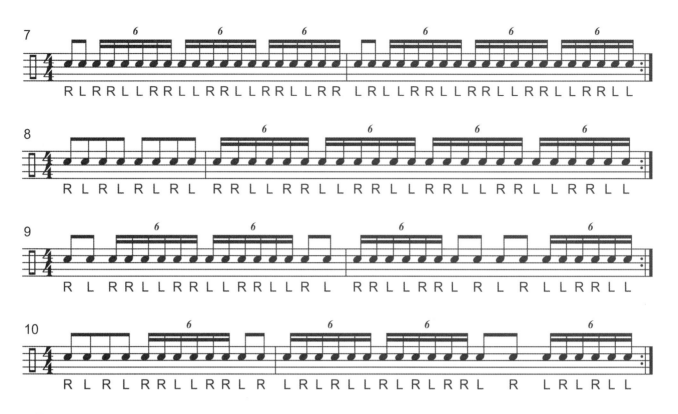

This exercise is like the previous one, but now we're using the double-paradiddle sticking on each group of six.

Here is yet another variation using the paradiddle-diddle sticking on each group of six. Be sure to try playing these starting with your left hand.

Finally, here's a variation of the first exercise using the multiple rebound (buzz) stroke. The idea is to get as many rebounds as possible while remaining relaxed. (Slightly increase your finger pressure on the buzz strokes.) This one is great for developing the closed roll.

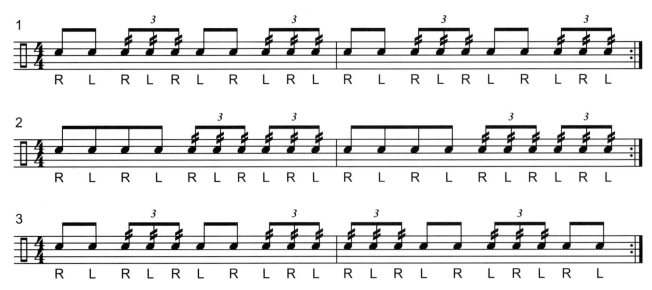

Paradiddle Combinations

The following exercises are great for developing control. Practice each one slowly at first, and remain relaxed at all times. Speed will come with slow, accurate practice. As your technical proficiency increases, you can increase the tempo setting on your metronome. These exercises can be played with or without accents.

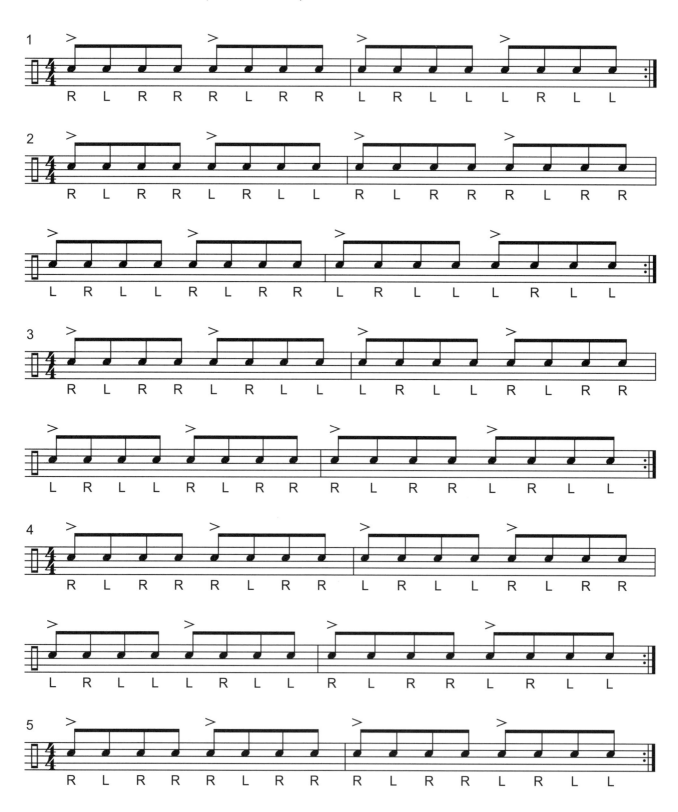

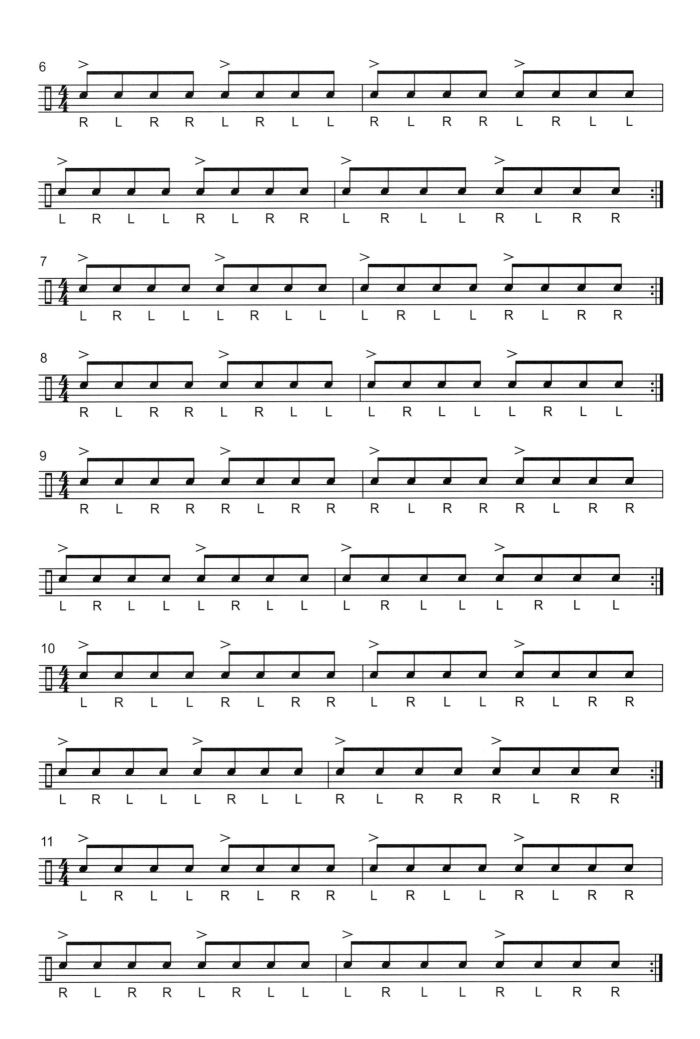

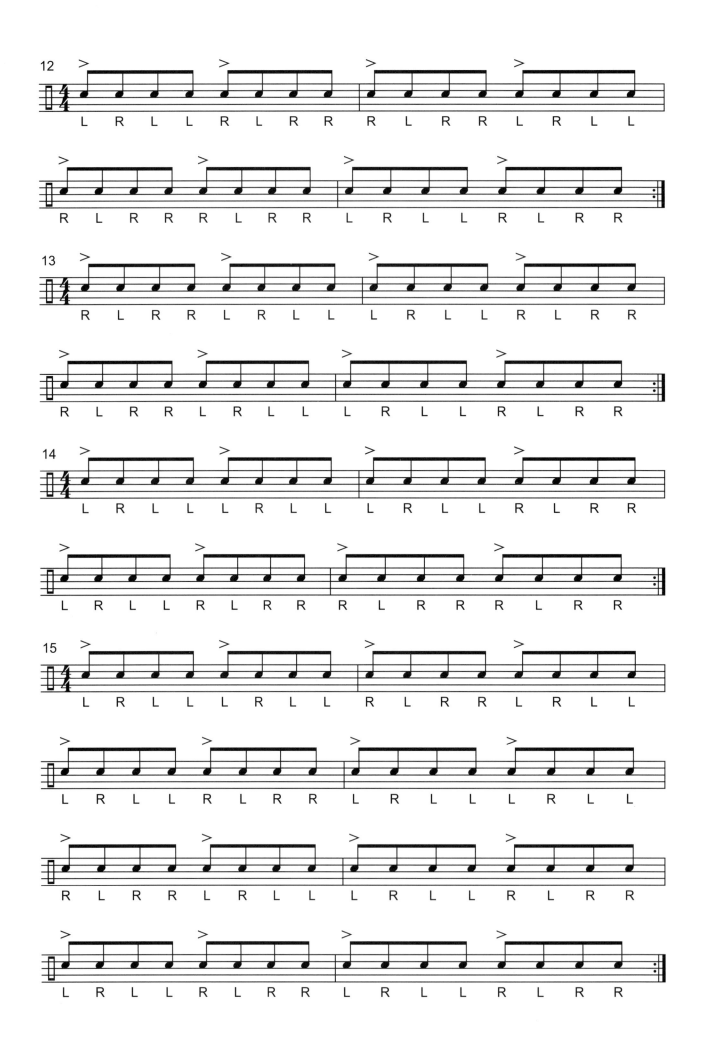

Paradiddles With Fill-Ins Using Single Strokes

This exercise builds upon the previous one. Now we have added fill-ins with single strokes. This exercise will help you build control as well as increase your ability to play a single-stroke roll. Again, practice each of these slowly at first, and focus on achieving accuracy.

Paradiddles With Fill-Ins Using Double Strokes

This exercise also builds upon the first one. Now we have added fill-ins with double strokes. This exercise will help you build control of the rebound stroke, thereby increasing your ability to play a double-stroke roll.

Paradiddles With Fill-Ins Using Multiple-Rebound Strokes

This exercise is also an elaboration on the first exercise. Now we've added multiple rebound (buzz) strokes. The object of this exercise is to get as many rebounds as possible while remaining relaxed at all times. This exercise will help you build control of the rebound stroke, thereby increasing your ability to play a closed roll.

Variations Of
The Triple Paradiddle

The following examples are designed for developing accent control. For an even greater challenge, you can play a flam on the first accent of each double stroke. These exer- cises can also be played on the drumset. Try playing the accented notes on the tom-toms while playing the unaccented notes on the snare drum.

Variations Of Triple Paradiddles With Fill-Ins

This exercise builds upon the previous one. Now we've added fill-ins. Play each one slowly at first. Once you begin to develop technical proficiency, increase the tempo setting on your metronome.

Variations Of Triple Paradiddles In Triplets

This exercise builds upon the previous exercises, only now we're using 8th-note triplets. These are also wonderful for developing accent control. I think you'll find them quite fun to play.

Variations Of Triple Paradiddles In Triplets With Fill-Ins

Now we've added fill-ins. Play each one slowly at first. As you gain technical proficiency, you can increase the tempo setting on your metronome.

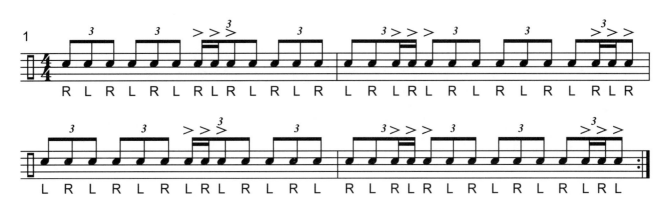

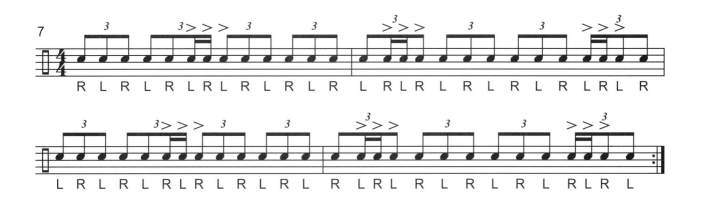

Triplet Variations

The following exercises are great for developing control. Play each of these slowly at first, and try to remain relaxed at all times. Again, speed will come with slow, accurate practice.

Once you've developed proficiency playing each one with accents, try playing them without accents. These exercises can also be played at varied dynamic levels.

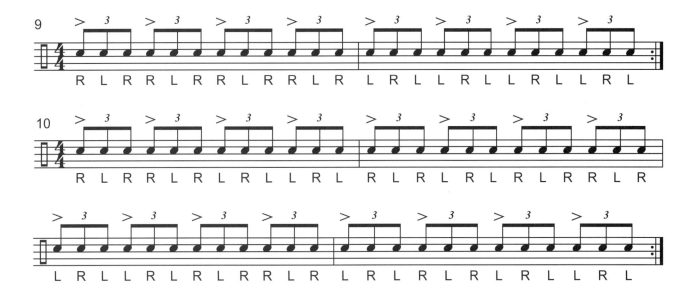

Triplet Variations With Fill-Ins Using Single Strokes

This exercise is based on the previous exercise. Now we're adding fill-ins with single strokes.

Triplet Variations With Fill-Ins Using Double Strokes

This exercise is also based on the first exercise. Now we're adding fill-ins with double strokes.

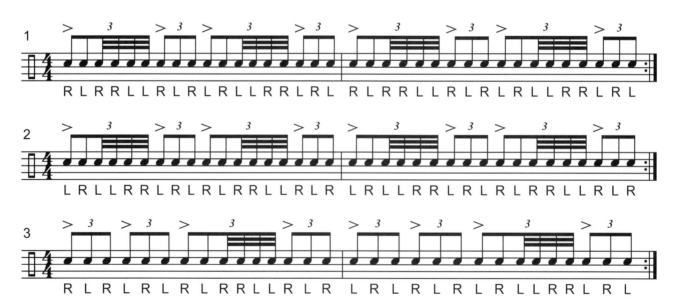

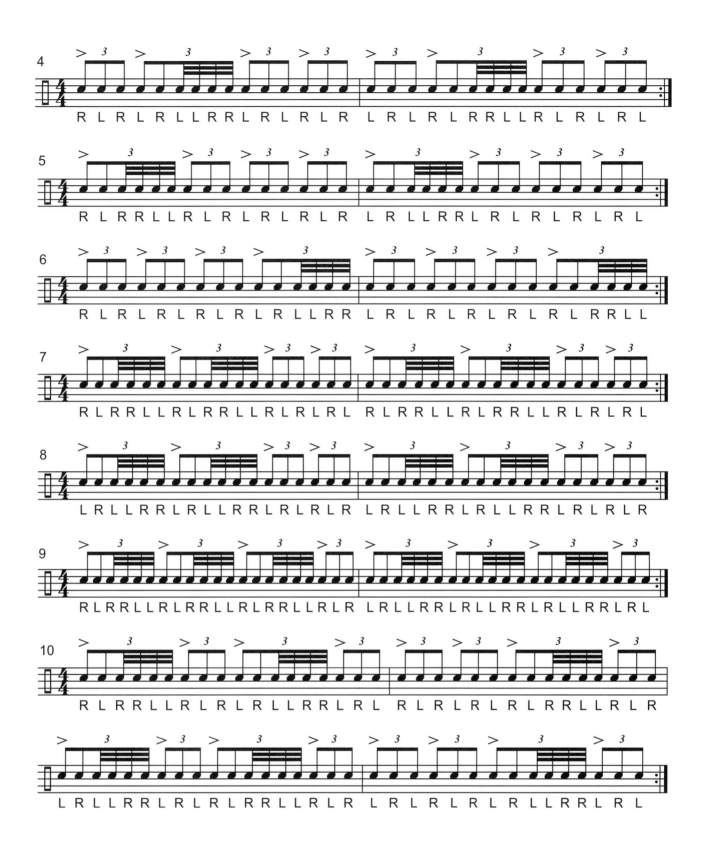

More Triplet Variations

Here are some triplet variations that can be played on the drumset and used as a basis for four-bar breaks in the jazz idiom. Try playing the accented notes on the tom-toms, bass drum, or cymbals while playing the unaccented notes on the snare drum. I would suggest practicing these exercises on a snare drum or practice pad before trying them on the drumset. Use your imagination to create some of your own patterns.

Endurance Exercise

The purpose of this exercise is to strengthen each hand individually in order to achieve a balance between the two. For the right-handed drummer, the left hand is the weaker hand, and vice versa. Play each one starting with your left hand, as shown, and then try them with your right. This exercise is great for developing the single-stroke roll.

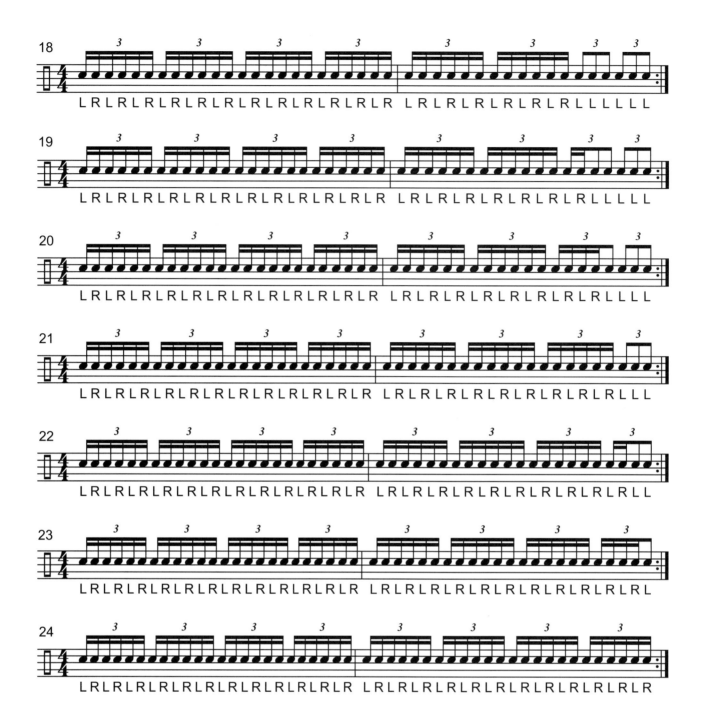

Joe Fingers

The following article was written by my teacher, the great George Lawrence Stone. It appeared in *International Musician* magazine many years ago. Here are Mr. Stone's words:

"The following is an old-timer from my private collection of practice routines, this one designed to develop speed plus endurance of the left (or weaker) hand. (For the lefty, it should be practiced with your weaker hand, which is the right.) This is dedicated to Joe Morello, for it was one of his favorites when studying here at The Stone School. Slow practice is indicated at first, with wrist action alone. Finger action is added when faster speeds are reached. Endurance is developed by

going through the set of ten exercises many times each, and finally, on a non-stop basis—that is, by going in this way from one number to another without a pause for, say, thirty minutes."

The first ten exercises shown below appeared in Mr. Stone's article. The next ten are my variations on his idea. I am sure Mr. Stone would be very pleased. He was one of the great teachers, and I was *so* honored to study with him. He really took me to another level of technical proficiency.

The key to understanding these exercises is recognizing that the hand motion (or sticking pattern) on the accents remains the same when you play the fill-ins.

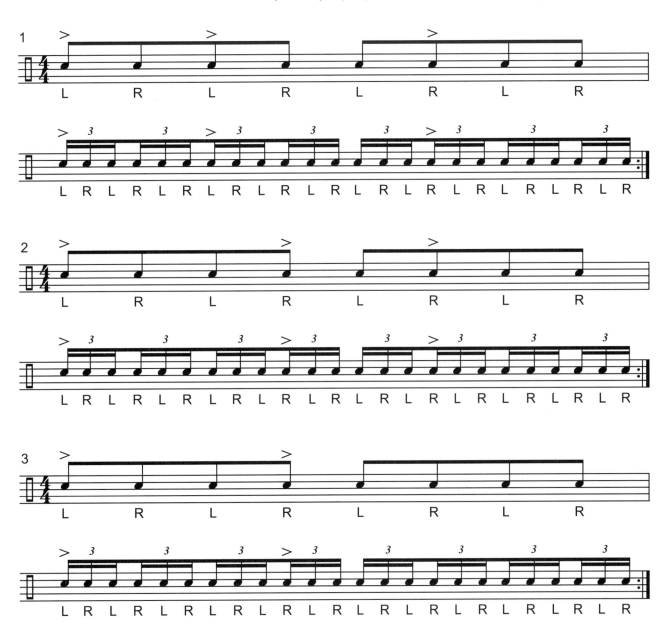

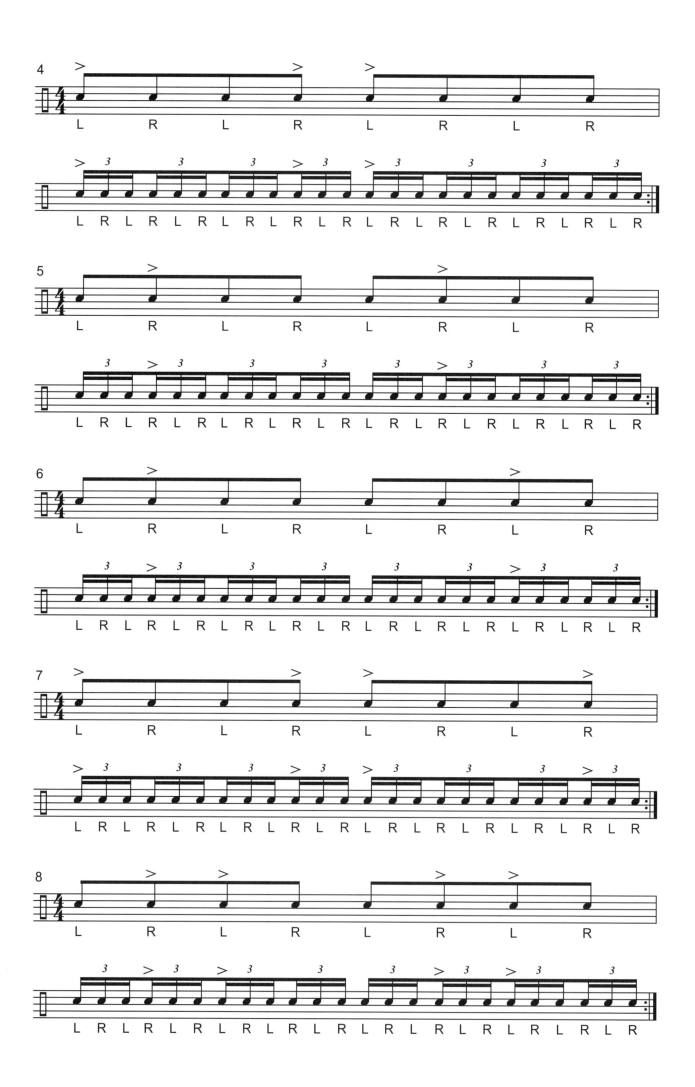

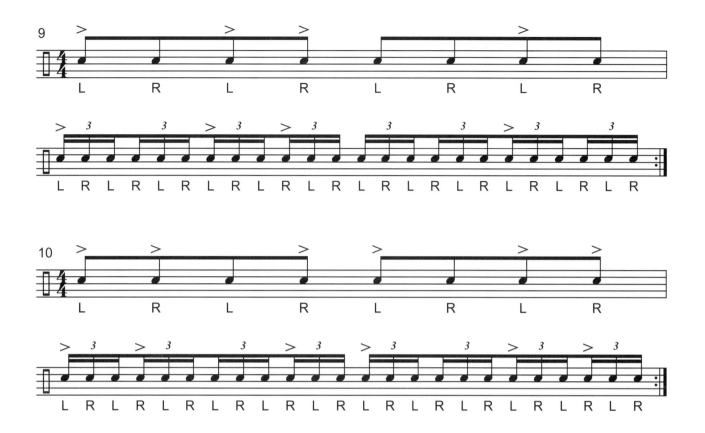

Here are my variations on Mr. Stone's exercises.

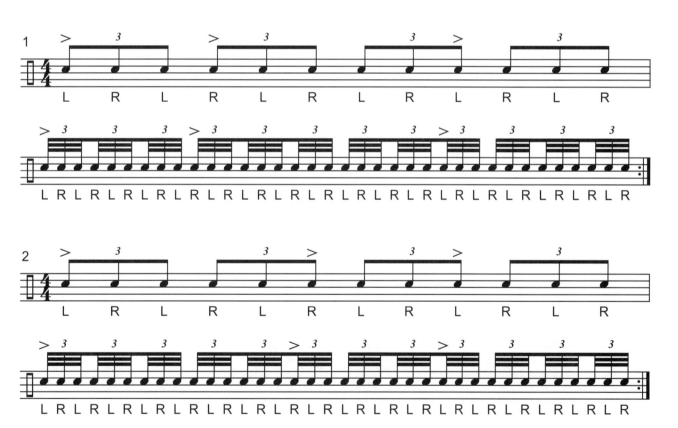

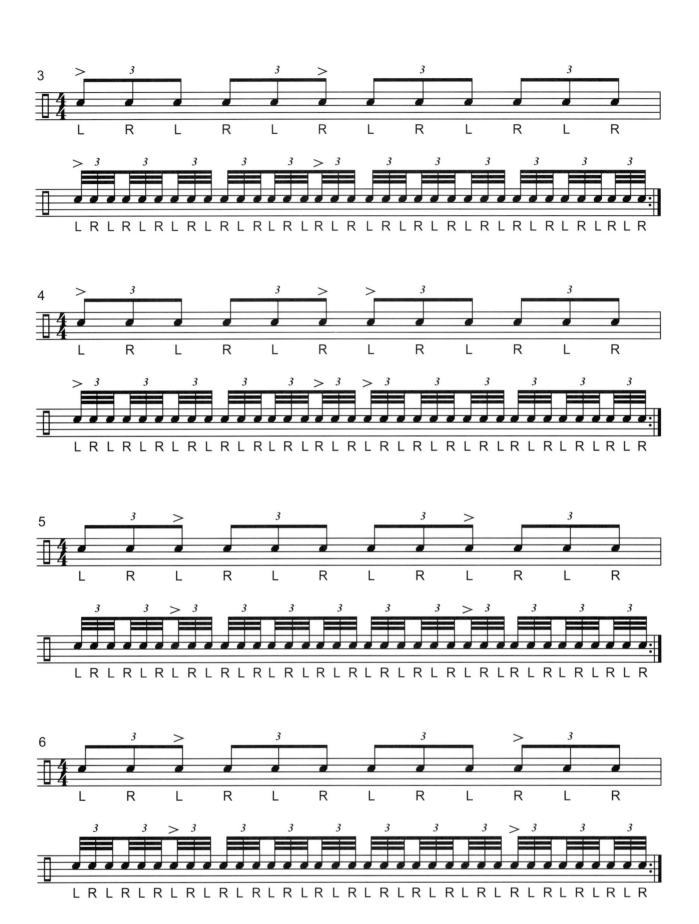

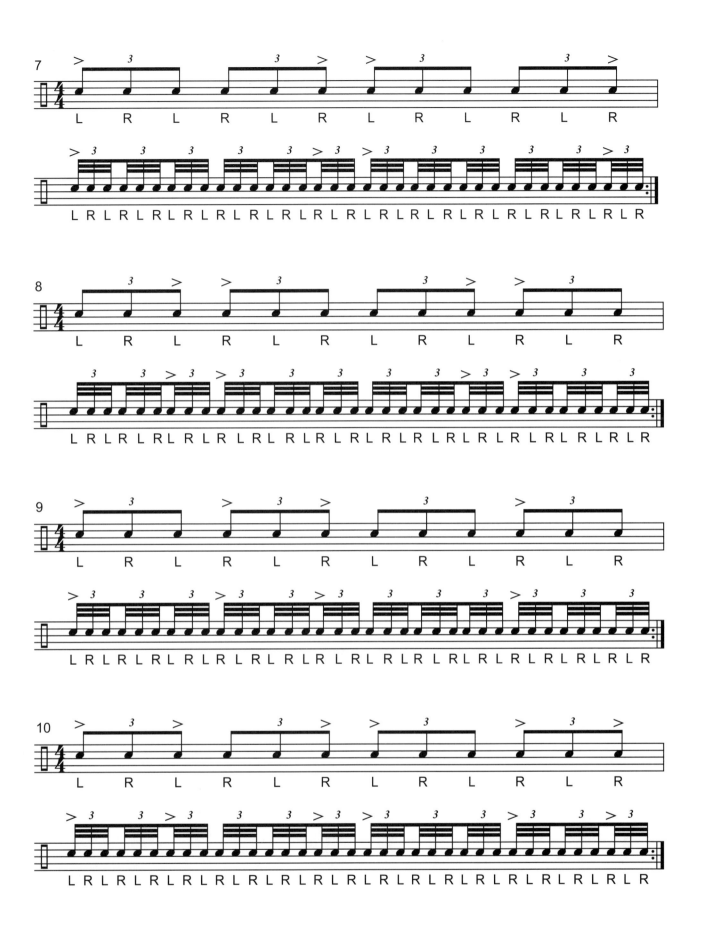

Control Studies

The purpose of these exercises is to gain control of playing accents in various parts of the triplet. You may find some of these to be quite difficult at first. However, with practice, the results will be very rewarding. As always, you should start out slowly and focus on achieving accuracy. Gradually increase the tempo setting on your metronome as you become more proficient at playing each exercise.

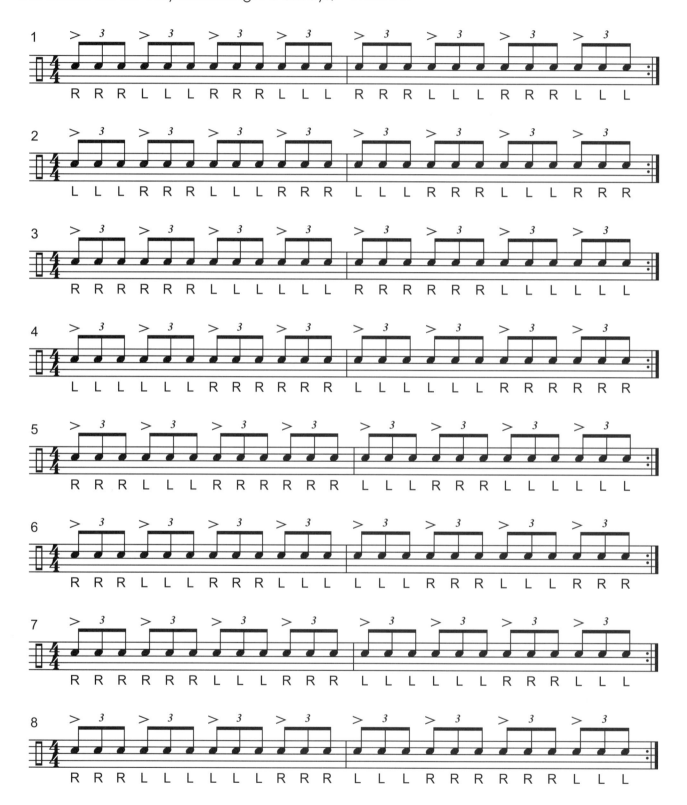

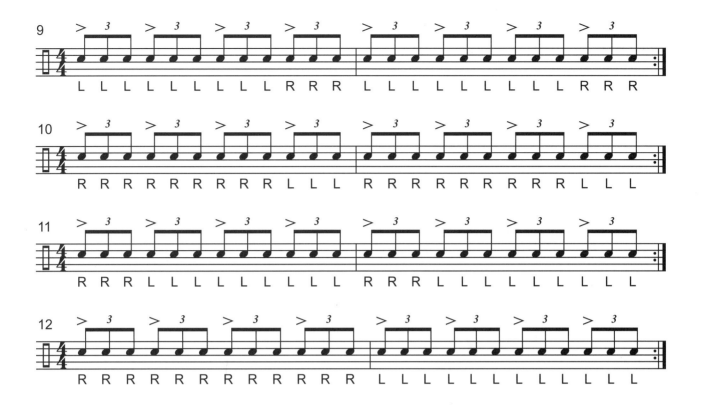

The accent is now on the middle note of each triplet.

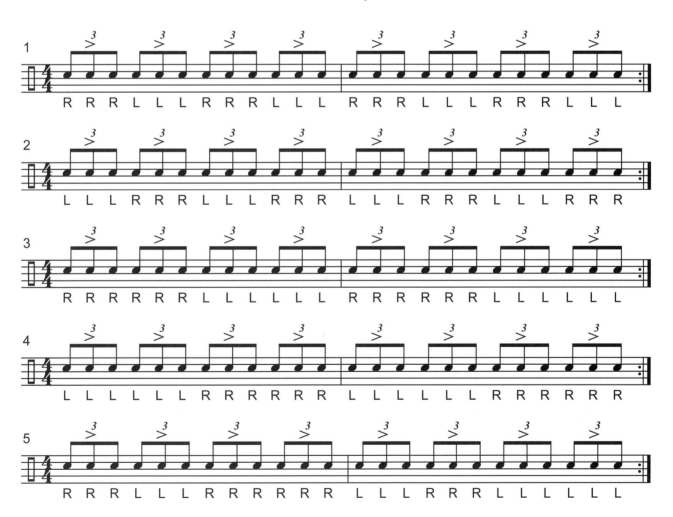

The accent is now on the last note of each triplet.

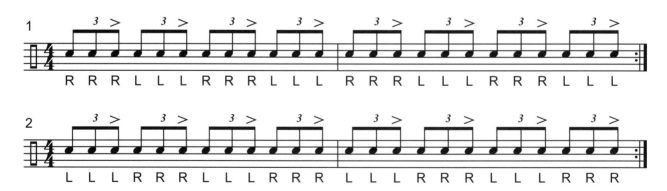

The accents are now on the first and middle notes of each triplet.

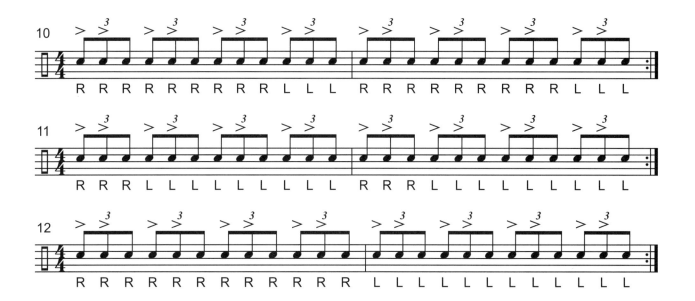

The accents are now on the middle and last notes of each triplet.

The accents are now on the first and last notes of each triplet.

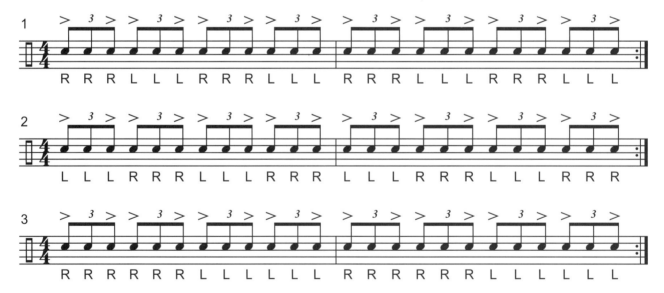

Control Studies With Fill-Ins

These exercises are based on the previous ones. Now we're adding fill-ins with single strokes. They will help you to further develop accent control, as well as build your single-stroke roll.

Remember to remain relaxed at all times. If any tension develops while you're playing, reduce the tempo setting on your metronome.

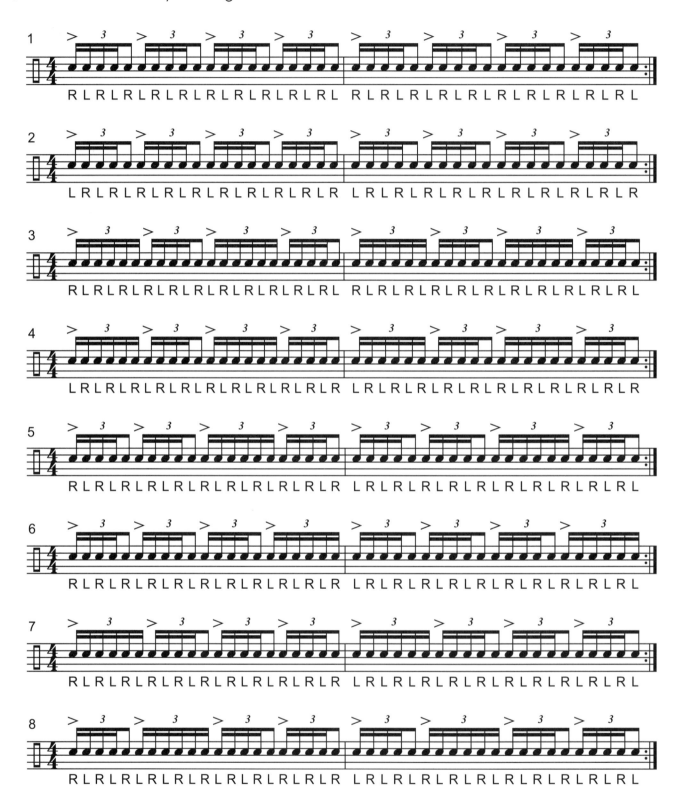

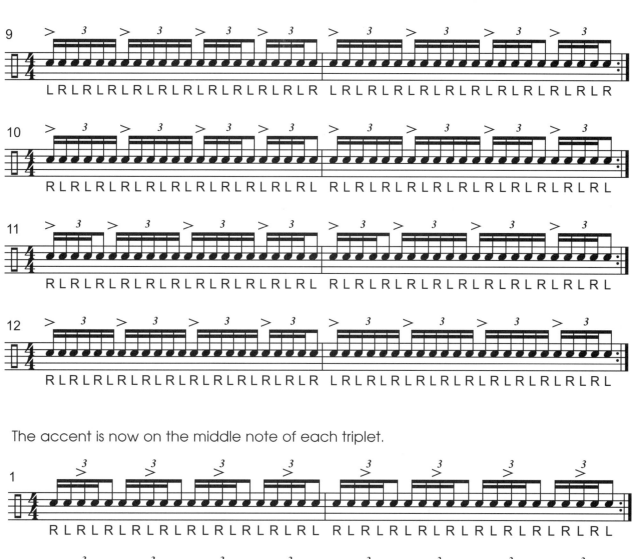

The accent is now on the middle note of each triplet.

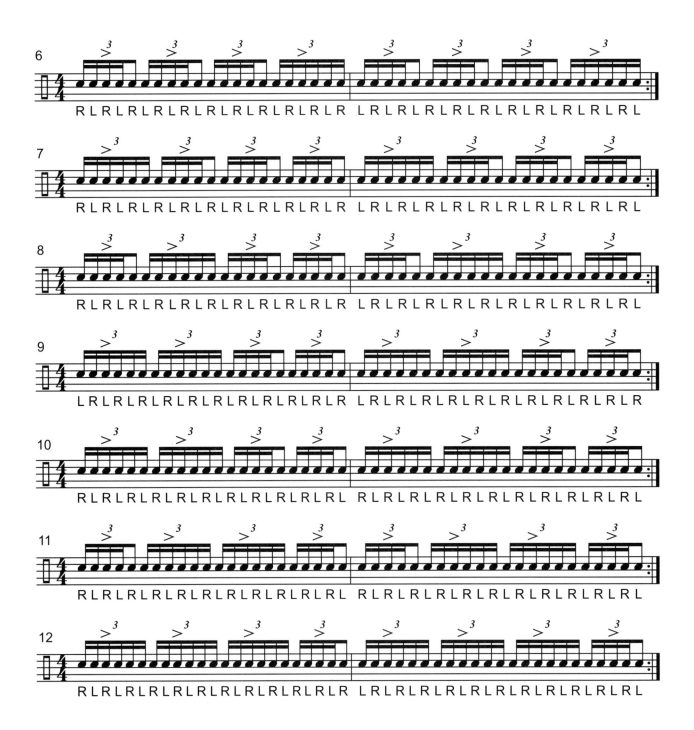

6

R L R L R L R L R L R L R L R L R L R L R L R L R L R L R L R L R L R L R L R L R L R L R L R L R L R L R L R L R L R L

7

R L R L R L R L R L R L R L R L R L R L R L R L R L R L R L R L R L R L R L R L R L R L R L R L R L R L R L R L R L R L

8

R L R L R L R L R L R L R L R L R L R L R L R L R L R L R L R L R L R L R L R L R L R L R L R L R L R L R L R L R L R L

9

L R L R L R L R L R L R L R L R L R L R L R L R L R L R L R L R L R L R L R L R L R L R L R L R L R L R L R L R L R L R

10

R L R L R L R L R L R L R L R L R L R L R L R L R L R L R L R L R L R L R L R L R L R L R L R L R L R L R L R L R L R L

11

R L R L R L R L R L R L R L R L R L R L R L R L R L R L R L R L R L R L R L R L R L R L R L R L R L R L R L R L R L R L

12

R L R L R L R L R L R L R L R L R L R L R L R L R L R L R L R L R L R L R L R L R L R L R L R L R L R L R L R L R L R L

The accent is now on the last note of each triplet.

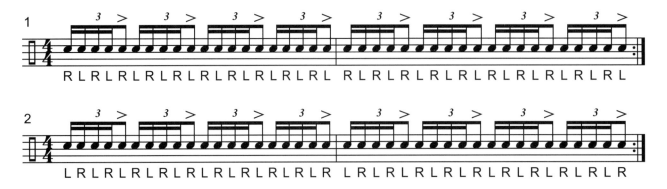

1

R L R L R L R L R L R L R L R L R L R L R L R L R L R L R L R L R L R L R L R L R L R L R L R L R L R L R L R L R L R L

2

L R L R L R L R L R L R L R L R L R L R L R L R L R L R L R L R L R L R L R L R L R L R L R L R L R L R L R L R L R L R

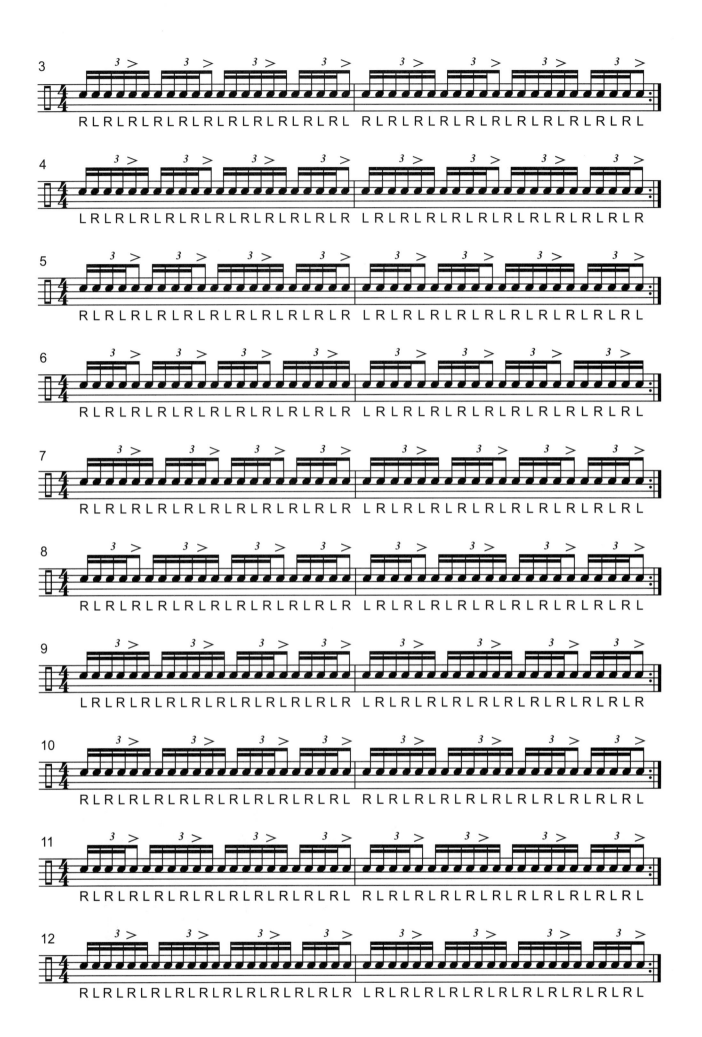

The accents are now on the first and middle notes of each triplet.

10

RLRLRLRLRLRLRLRLRLRLRLRL RLRLRLRLRLRLRLRLRLRLRLRL

11

RLRLRLRLRLRLRLRLRLRLRLRL RLRLRLRLRLRLRLRLRLRLRLRL

12

RLRLRLRLRLRLRLRLRLRLRLRL LRLRLRLRLRLRLRLRLRLRLRLR

The accents are now on the middle and last notes of each triplet.

1

RLRLRLRLRLRLRLRLRLRLRLRL RLRLRLRLRLRLRLRLRLRLRLRL

2

LRLRLRLRLRLRLRLRLRLRLRLR LRLRLRLRLRLRLRLRLRLRLRLR

3

RLRLRLRLRLRLRLRLRLRLRLRL RLRLRLRLRLRLRLRLRLRLRLRL

4

LRLRLRLRLRLRLRLRLRLRLRLR LRLRLRLRLRLRLRLRLRLRLRLR

5

RLRLRLRLRLRLRLRLRLRLRLRL LRLRLRLRLRLRLRLRLRLRLRLR

6

RLRLRLRLRLRLRLRLRLRLRLRL LRLRLRLRLRLRLRLRLRLRLRLR

61

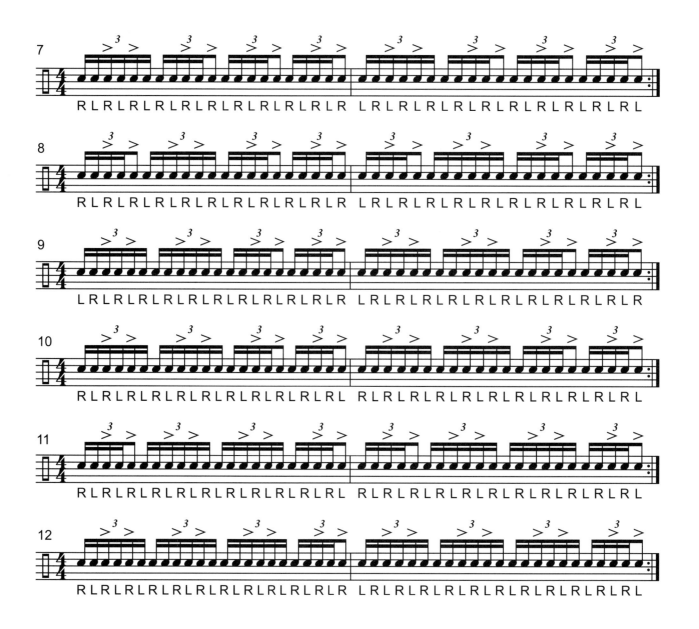

The accents are now on the first and last notes of each triplet.

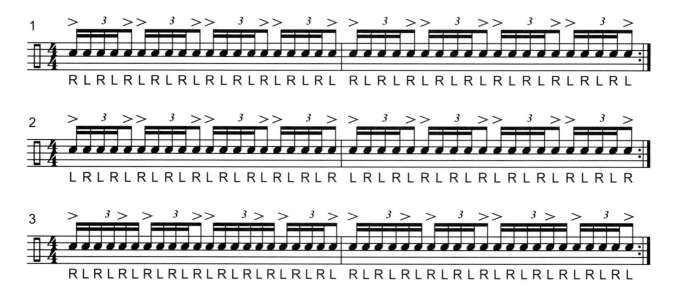

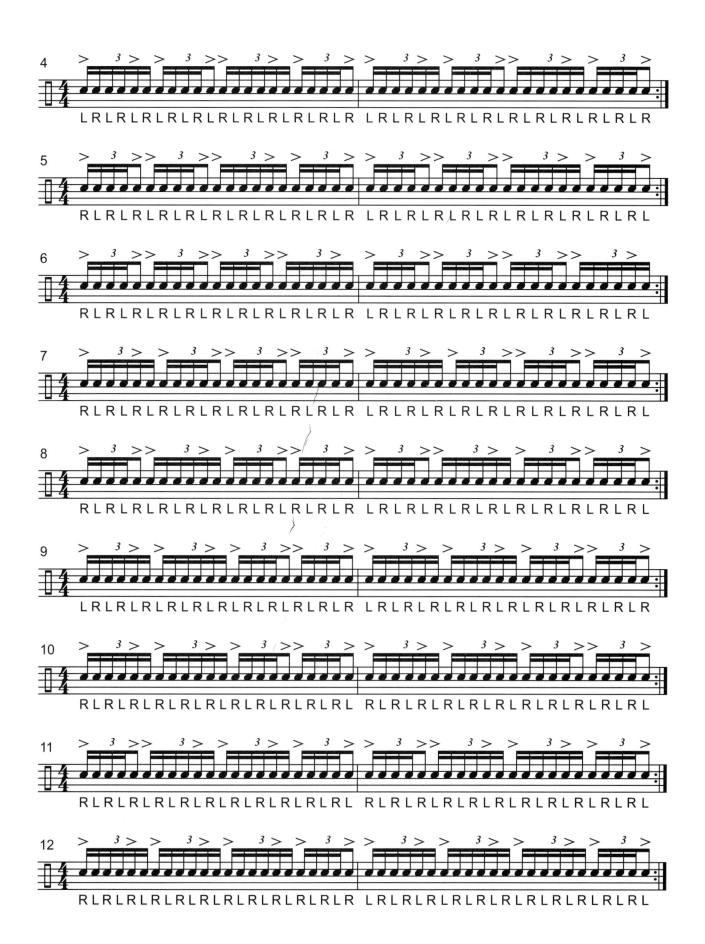

Developing The Single-Stroke Roll

The following exercises are designed to build your single-stroke roll using different groupings. I think you'll find these quite interesting. Play each exercise with accents, as indicated, and then try them without accents. Feel free to play these at varied dynamic levels. Also, try them starting with your left hand.

Groups Of Four And Six

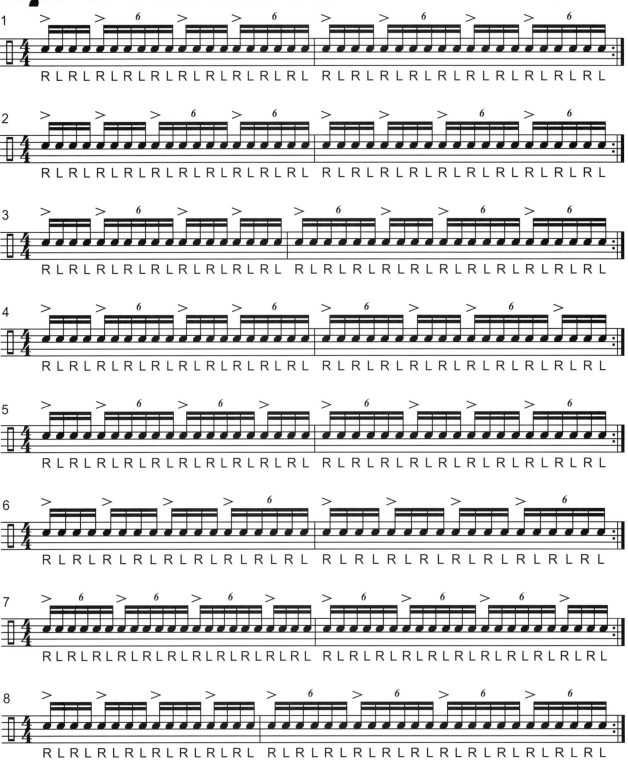

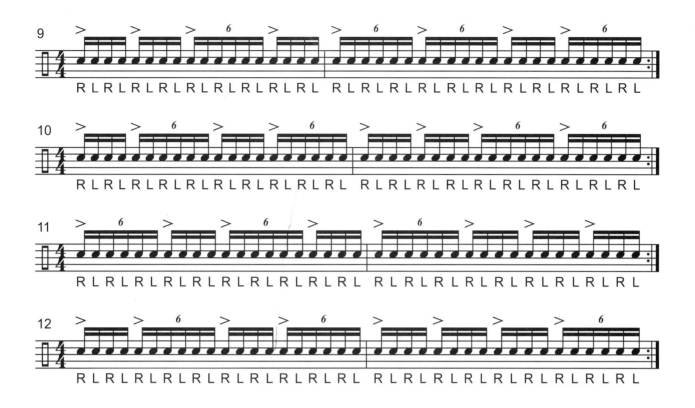

Groups Of Four And Five

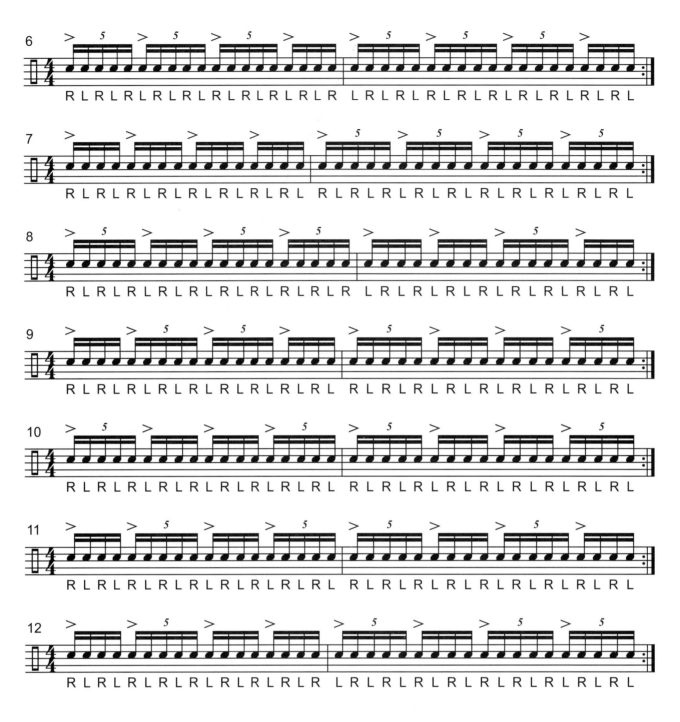

Groups Of Five And Six

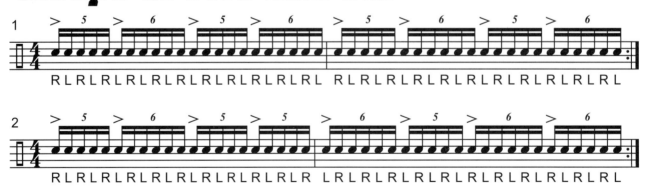

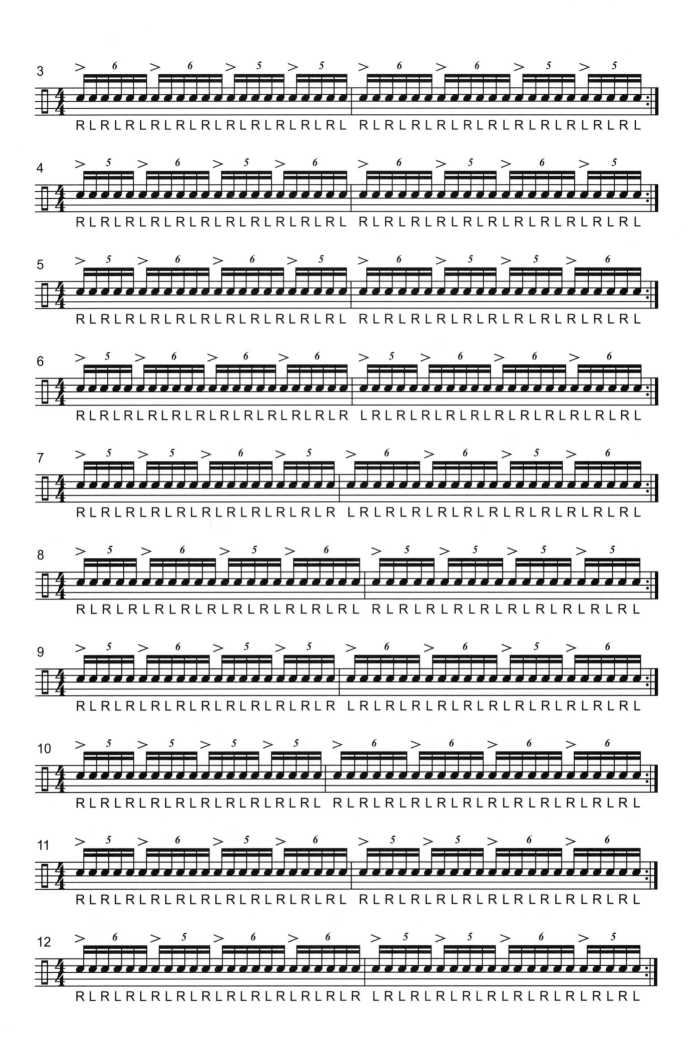

Groups Of Three And Five

Groups Of Five And Seven

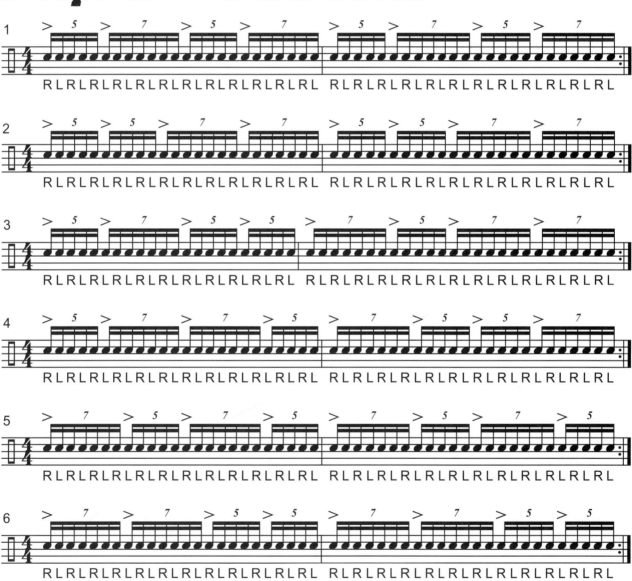

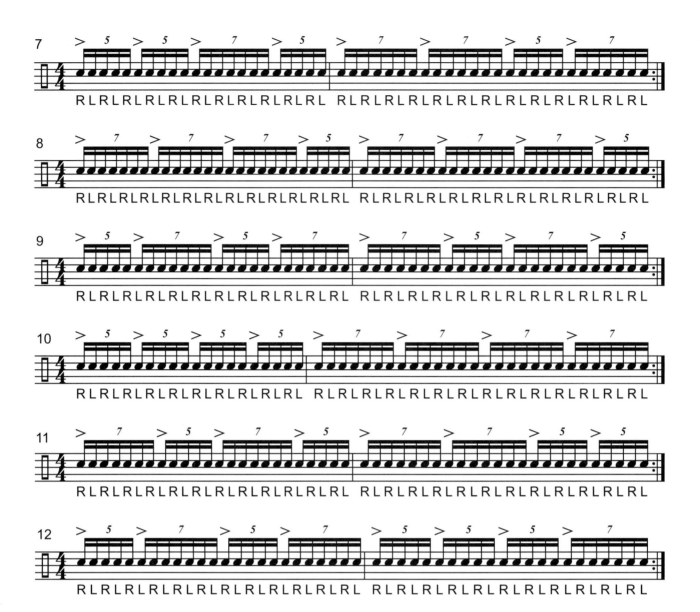

Table Of Time (Revisited)

Here is a great exercise that requires considerable "mental dexterity." The object is to be able to play three within four, four within five, five within six, etc. In other words, accent every third note in a group of four, every fourth note in a group of five, every fifth note in a group of six, and so on. Start out slowly at first, and be sure to use a metronome. I think you'll find this one to be very challenging.

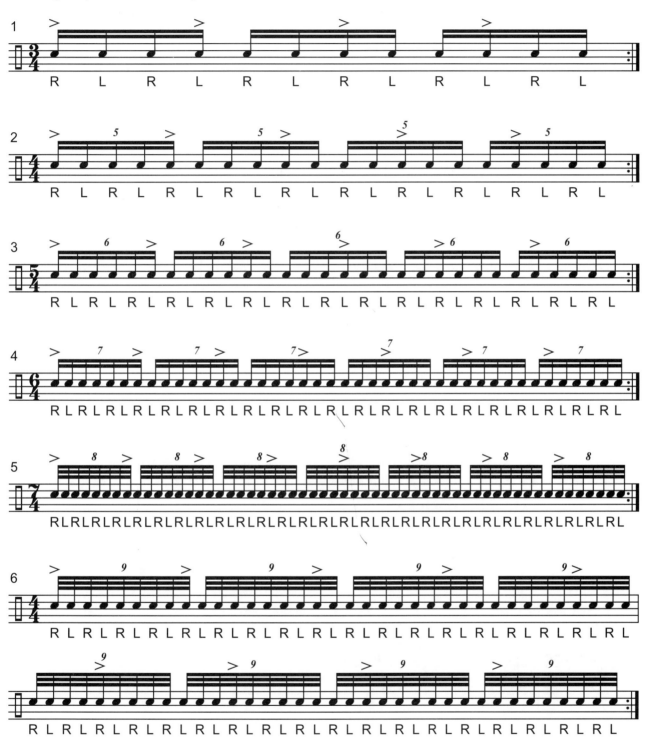

Sticking Variations In Groups Of Five

These exercises are designed to increase your ability to play in groups of five using a variety of sticking patterns. These are very difficult, so start out slowly. First, play each one without accents. Then be creative and add them. These exercises can also be played on the drumset. For example, play each right on the tom-toms and each left on the snare drum.

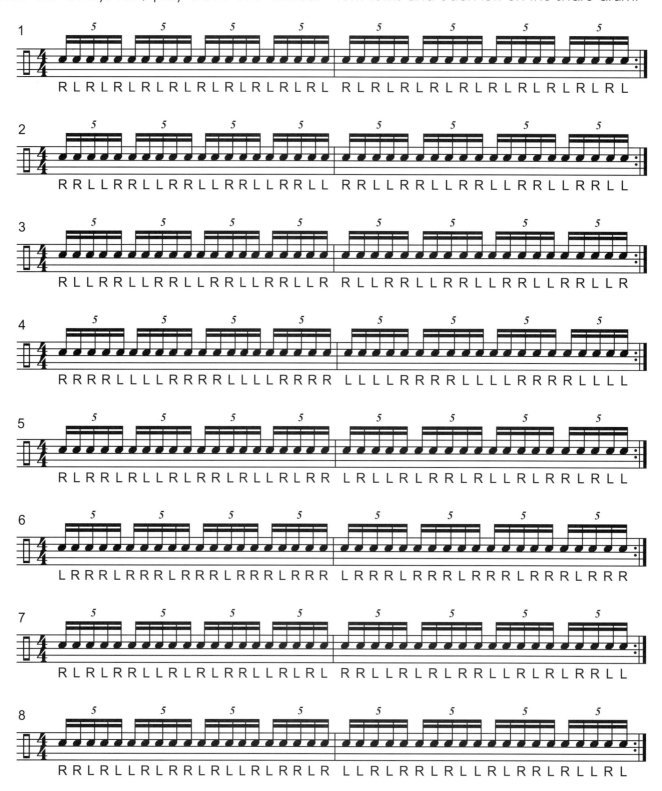

1 R L R L R L R L R L R L R L R L R L R L   R L R L R L R L R L R L R L R L R L R L

2 R R L L R R L L R R L L R R L L R R L L   R R L L R R L L R R L L R R L L R R L L

3 R L L R R L L R R L L R R L L R R L L R   R L L R R L L R R L L R R L L R R L L R

4 R R R L L L L R R R R L L L L R R R R   L L L L R R R R L L L L R R R R L L L L

5 R L R R L R L L R L R R L R L L R L R R   L R L L R L R R L R L L R L R R L R L L

6 L R R R L R R R L R R R L R R R L R R R   L R R R L R R R L R R R L R R R L R R R

7 R L R L R R L L R L R L R R L L R L R L   R R L L R L R L R R L L R L R L R R L L

8 R R L R L L R L R R L R L L R L R R L R   L L R L R R L R L L R L R R L R L L L R L

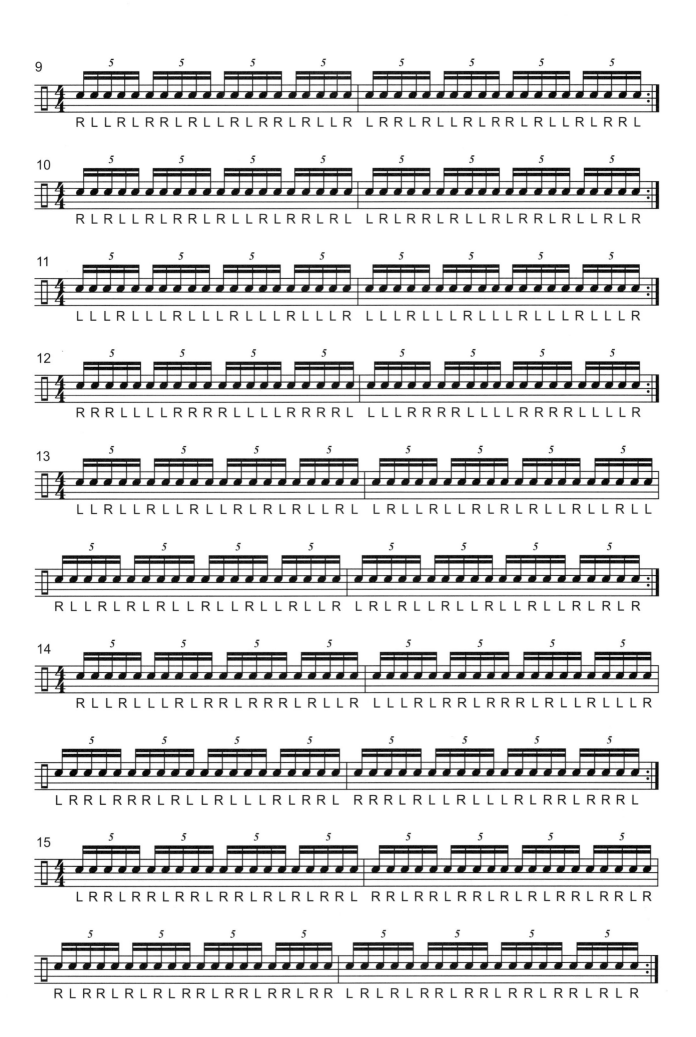

Sticking Variations In Groups Of Seven

These exercises are designed to increase your ability to play in groups of seven using a variety of sticking patterns. They are *extremely* difficult, so start out slowly. First, play each one without accents, as indicated, and then use your imagination and add them. These can also be played on the drumset. For example, play each right on the tom-toms and each left on the snare drum.

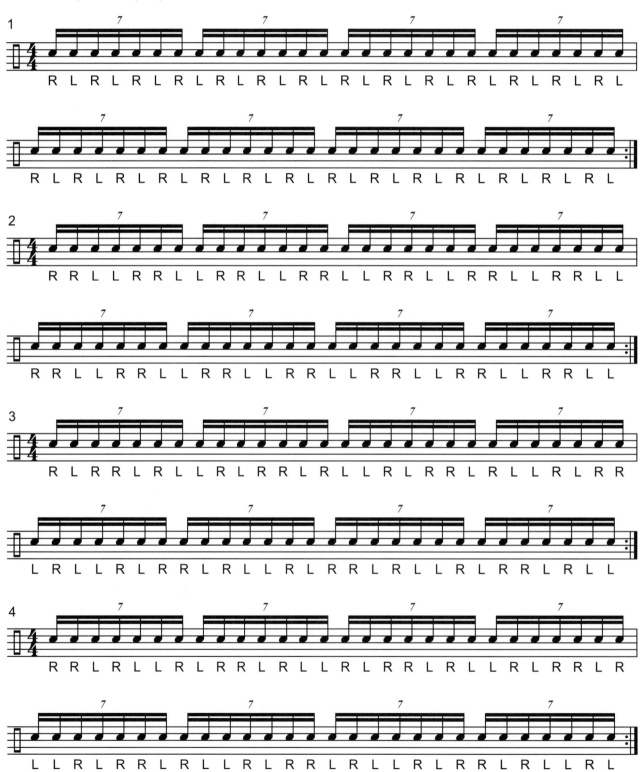

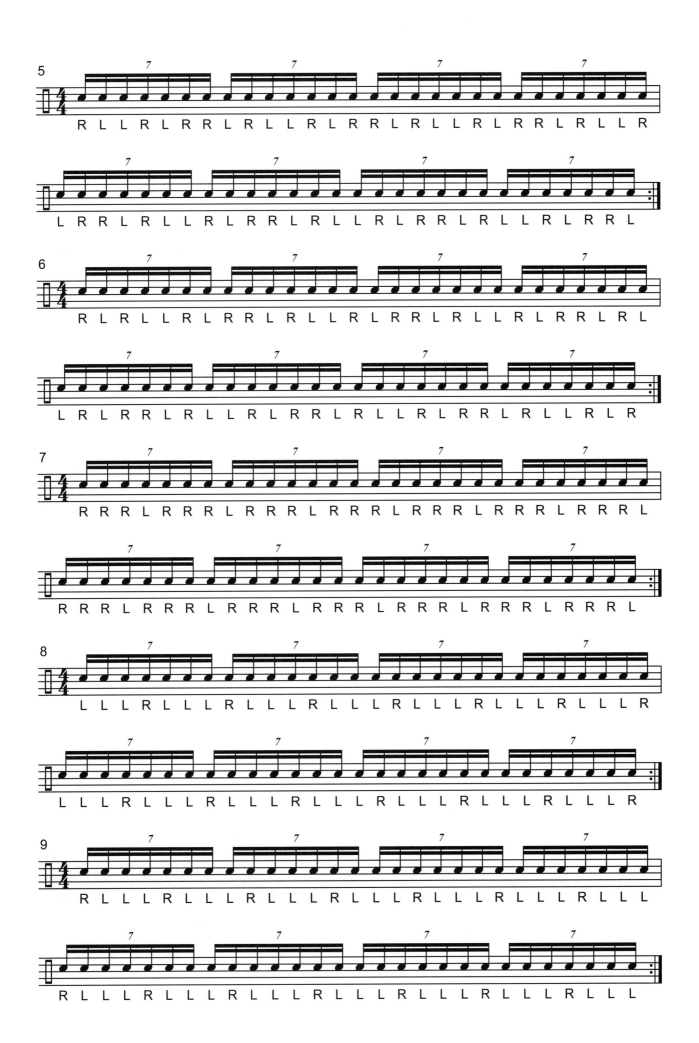

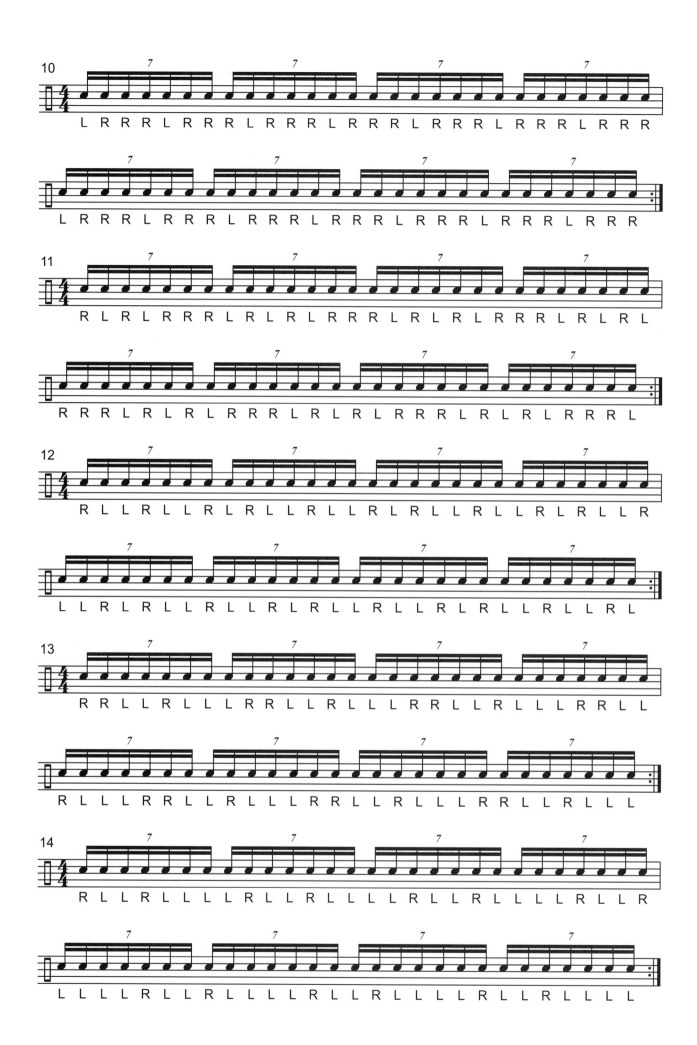

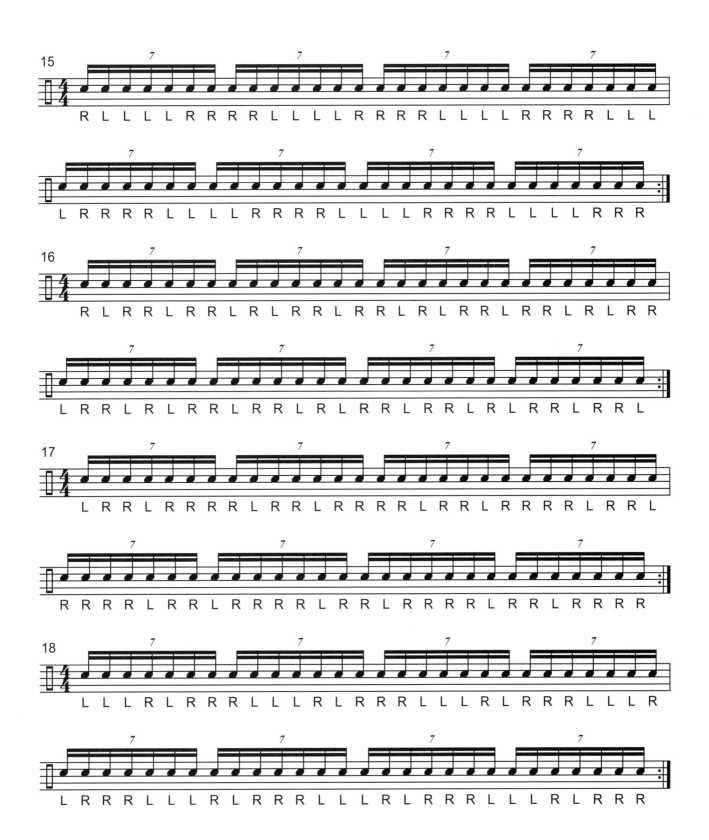

Adventure In Time

This is going to be a challenge for drummers who are accustomed to playing in 4/4 time. These exercises are based on the "8th Notes With Accents" section of *Master Studies*. The original version is shown above each example. The first group of exercises has been modified using different time signatures. The second group uses different time signatures and note values. These exercises are designed to give you a feel for playing over the barline. I am sure these will broaden your rhythmic horizons.

Biography

A young Joe Morello, from his early days in New York in the 1950s.

Morello with The Dave Brubeck Quartet, one of the most successful jazz groups of all time.

Joe has traveled the world, both as a performer and clinician. This press shot was taken in Ceylon (current day Sri Lanka).

Joe Morello was born on July 17, 1928, in Springfield, Massachusetts. Having impaired vision since birth, he devoted himself to indoor activities. At the age of six, his family's encouragement led him to studying the violin. Three years later, he was featured with the Boston Symphony Orchestra as soloist in the "Mendelssohn Violin Concerto." At the age of twelve, he made a second solo appearance with this orchestra. But upon meeting and hearing his idol, the great Jascha Heifetz, Joe felt he could never achieve "that sound." So at the age of fifteen, Joe changed the course of his musical endeavors and began to study drums.

Joe's first drum teacher, Joe Sefcik, was a pit drummer for all of the shows in the Springfield area. Sefcik was an excellent teacher and gave Joe much encouragement. Joe began sitting in with any group that would allow it. When he was not sitting in, he and his friends, including Chuck Andrus, Hal Sera, Phil Woods, and Sal Salvador, would get together and jam anyplace they could find. Joe would play any job he was called for. As a result, his musical experiences ranged from rudimental military playing to weddings and social occasions. Eventually, Mr. Sefcik decided it was time for Joe to move on. He recommended a teacher in Boston, the great George Lawrence Stone.

Mr. Stone did many things for Joe. He gave Joe most of the tools for developing technique. He taught Joe to read. But probably most important of all, he made Joe realize his future was in jazz, not legitimate percussion as Joe had hoped. Through his studies with Mr. Stone, Joe became known as the best drummer in Springfield and rudimental champion of New England.

Joe's playing activity increased, and he soon found himself on the road with several groups. First, there was Hank Garland and the Grand Ole Opry, and then Whitey Bernard. After much consideration, Joe left Whitey Bernard to go to New York City.

Joe today

William Ostenfeld

The masters meet: Joe with friends Billy Cobham (above) and Buddy Rich.

Jeff Felder

A difficult year followed, but with Joe's determination and the help of friends like Sal Salvador, Joe began to be noticed. Soon he found himself playing with an impressive cast of musicians that included Gil Melle, Johnny Smith, Tal Farlow, Jimmy Raney, Stan Kenton, and Marian McPartland. After leaving Marian McPartland's trio, he turned down offers from Benny Goodman and Tommy Dorsey's bands . The offer he chose to accept was a two-month temporary tour with The Dave Brubeck Quartet, which ended up lasting twelve and a half years. It was during this period that Joe's technique received its finishing touches from Billy Gladstone of Radio City Music Hall fame.

Since 1968, when The Dave Brubeck Quartet disbanded, Joe has spread his talents over a variety of areas. He maintains a very active private teaching practice. Through his association with the Ludwig drum company, and now with DW drums and Sabian cymbals, Joe has made great educational contributions to drumming, as well as the entire field of jazz by way of his clinics, lectures, and guest solo appearances. Joe also performs with his own trio and quartet.

Joe has appeared on over one hundred twenty-five albums, of which sixty were with The Dave Brubeck Quartet. He won the *Down Beat* award for five years in a row and the *Playboy* award for seven years in a row, and he is the only drummer to win every major music magazine poll for five years in a row, including those in Japan, England, Europe, Australia, and South America. He is mentioned in *Who's Who In The East* and the *Blue Book*, which is a listing of persons in the United Kingdom, Ireland, Canada, Australia, New Zealand, and the United States who have achieved distinction in the arts, sciences, business, or the professions. Joe is also a recipient of the *Modern Drummer*, American Jazz, and Percussive Arts Society Hall Of Fame Awards, as well as the Thomas A. Edison, Berklee College of Music, KoSA International Percussion, and Sabian Lifetime Achievement Awards. Revered by fans and musicians alike, Joe is considered to be one of the finest, and is certainly one of the most celebrated, drummers in the history of jazz.

Joe was one of the most in-demand clinicians of the 1960s and '70s, averaging thirty clinics a year all around the world.